STANDING IN THE GAP

The Mayo Writers' Block

An Anthology

Edited By Terry McDonagh.

STANDING IN THE GAP
The Mayo Writers' Block – An Anthology.

First published 2007.
Sionnach Media,
47 Grace Park Meadows, Drumcondra, Dublin 9, Ireland.
www.sionnach-media.com

A catalogue record for this title is
available from the British Library.

ISBN-13: 978-0-9553804-1-9
ISBN-10: 0-9553804-1-3

Printed in Ireland by ColourBooks Ltd., Baldoyle Industrial Estate, Dublin 13.

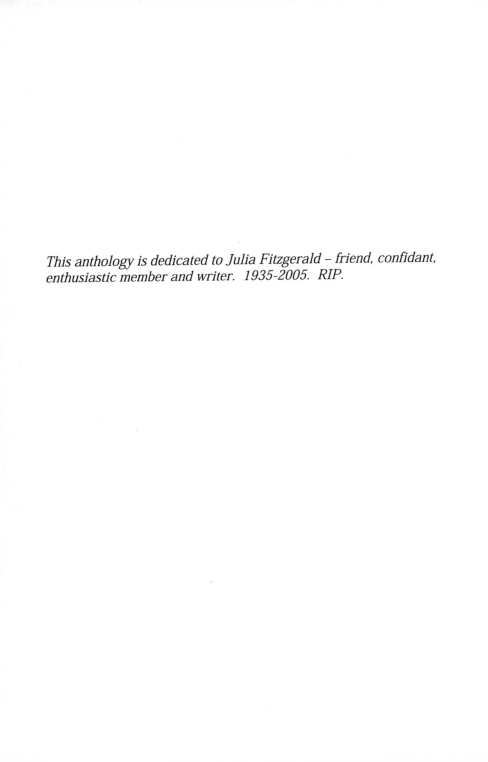

This anthology is dedicated to Julia Fitzgerald – friend, confidant, enthusiastic member and writer. 1935-2005. RIP.

Contents

Foreword

The written word allows us a glimpse into the minds and hearts of people in a society at a particular point in history; it is a kind of barometer measuring climate of opinion. The arts don't always have the answers, but they do address themes like loneliness, old age, nostalgia, failed relationships, or the need for human interaction in its broadest sense. There's an opportunity to challenge; to be contrary; to be subversive in principle; to poke fun at self, and to question the pillars of society.

The Mayo Writers' Block is made up of a tireless retinue of men and women who have been meeting twice a month for the past three years to put their thoughts on paper and exchange insights and ideas. The outcome is impressive. In addition to their own work, they invite a constant flow of visiting writers to share their experiences of publishing, performance and pitfalls.

This is a powerful anthology of stories, poetry and film scripts. There is something special for every reader and one feels the group is at a very potent chapter in its relatively short history.

The Mayo Writers' Block has a life out-on-its-own and it has, now, a permanent record of its achievements. Congratulations to all who have had the courage to contribute.

Terry McDonagh

Wordaholics

The impact of those framed words of Richard Burton (1880) would stay with her the rest of her days. As she committed them to her notebook a voice at her elbow said:

'Impressed?'

'Yes,' on two counts, mentally noting the intruder's good looks. She scribbled madly as people rushed past her up and down the stairs. *'Concentrate,'* she lectured herself ensuring that the 'no's and the 'knows nots' were in the right places.

How fortunate to find such a neat philosophy of life on this her first day at university, where people could be divided into four groups: the foolish, the simple, sleepyheads and the wise. How daunting. Nevertheless, it should be fun sorting them. A glance at her watch impelled her through the door of her first class of the day, English. She was last in.

'Ah you have to be Miss Kane.'

'Yes,' she said, sliding into the only empty seat.

'J-u-l-i-a'

'Correct,' and she juggled her books.

'Perhaps, Julia, you'd care to share those words of wisdom I saw you copy and get us started on a philosophical note.'

Was it not bad enough being late? Why should she get the class started when he was being paid to do so? Now all eyes were upon her once more. Blushing, she stood as straight as she could and tried to read slowly, loudly and clearly:

'He who knows not and knows not he knows not, he is a fool, shun him. He who knows not and knows he knows not, he is simple, teach him. He who knows and knows not he knows, he is asleep, wake him. He who knows and knows he knows, he is wise, follow him.'

Resuming her seat she gave him a forbidding look, which was not lost on him.

Class did get off to a good start but came to a better end. Mr. Ravishing thanked her for her contribution and apologised for putting her on the spot. He walked her to her next class and invited her to join the Scrabble Club. That was the beginning of a romance

11

that would last a lifetime. Both were wordaholics, in love with the English language.

Doggone Kangaroo

You may laugh, sneer, jibe or condemn. What's new? People, of his time, did all that to Christopher Columbus.

'You'll fall off the edge,' they cautioned him. I, too, have been warned: *those in the know will pour scorn on your theories. Who? The experts, of course.*

Good. Let them prove me wrong. Anything to get the media off politics, gloom and disaster.

So come on experts, take a serious look at my contention that the kangaroo derived from the dog.

It is believed that today's Australian Aboriginals moved there from New Guinea about 40,000 years ago. Except for native fauna they found a vast uninhabited land with unpolluted seas abounding in marine life and crystal clear fresh waters teeming with fish. Nature was at its abundant best so they set about living in harmony with such bounty, taking only enough of anything for each day.

Although the dogs they took with them as pets and helpers were fast they were no match for the continent's fauna. The settlers attempted to train the dogs to catch low-flying insects and birds – even to fish in the billabongs. With great patience on the part of the tribesmen and much effort by the dogs, the new skills were gradually mastered. But eating the catch had to be discouraged and eventually eliminated. To this end a reward system was used. Each time an intact fish or bird was brought in, non-carnivorous morsels were awarded accompanied by much praise and patting. (Now we know where Pavlov got his ideas.) In time the dogs became herbivores and grazed contentedly. This of course took a very long time.

Bushfires, the greatest danger threatened both habitat and food supply for all. Hindered by the fires in their pursuit of ground animals, the dogs, already adept at leaping after prey, perfected the skill - their strides becoming longer and their leaps higher. Little by little they developed a kind of hop and began to stand or rest on their hind legs. This new stride and posture enabled them to see better, reach higher and move with greater agility when chasing prey or escaping danger.

With practise the movement became habitual. Less use of the front legs over a vast time scale led to their shortening. Stronger, hind legs developed, as did a longer, thicker tail for greater balance. Now they were better equipped to see bushfires and find food for themselves and their masters. They became, in fact, the island's fastest animal because they had adapted to their environment and its needs as well as their own. Over hundreds of thousands of years the descendants of those original dogs evolved into what were first called 'doggaroos'. Today they are known as kangaroos.

This could be the origin of the term 'doggone': dog gone. My hypotheses are no more preposterous than the big bang theory, are they? In any case, the kangaroo, so named by the Aborigines, is one of Australia's best known and most admired animal.

Your People

They're proud people,
your people. Don't forget that.
And staunch.

No-one ever starved
who lived beside the long meadow.

A mountain of shells
on the side of a mountain,
a testament

hidden like the ashes,
Round The Shore.

He was a stout man,
he held friendship.

A generation removed
from abstract poverty.

He raised   a phoenix.

Old

Old is something I don't want to be
Struggling to move about – problems with my knee
Struggling to contain myself – I really need a wee
Struggling to watch TV – I cannot even see
Struggling to remember – how to count to three
Struggling 'cause I'm lonely – my family's forgotten me
Struggling with shaky hands – and spilling all my tea
Struggling with the pension – the government stole from me.
Struggling, always struggling – while the youths look on in glee
Yes old is something that we all don't think we'll be.

Loneliness

I am the people who listen and never hear
in corridors and corners and dark, busy places,
filling rooms.
I am the clink of glasses and laughter
that eludes you.
I am the expert who smiles politely with no comment.
I am the doctor, the parent, and the friends who tell you
nothing is wrong and how lucky you are.

I am the silence that follows the slam of the front door
and the person beside you on the couch,
staring ahead.
I am the smile that cracks cheekbones, burning eyelids
and the tearful friend who rings at 2am and
never asks if they disturbed you.

I am the reflection in the mirror and the eyes
you never meet.
I am each patronising relative
you speak to from the corner of a room.
I am all the words you never quite say,
and the hands you raised that never got noticed.

I am a solitary cigarette smoked at midnight
from the bedroom window,
and mumbling radio voices playing long into the night.
I am a desk of paperwork and decisions you try
to sound confident in making.
I am every choice that you pretend to understand.

I am the television guide on a Saturday night
and a bottle and glass hidden under the kitchen sink
when the doorbell rings.
I am an engaged tone on the telephone,
the bright face gazing out of a window,

and the voice that says you like your own company.

I am eyes that read things in other people,
then wish they hadn't.
I am the one who holds you back in dark times
to keep you calm and quiet.
I am a sigh when the party is over
and a welcome mat left outside the back door.

The Loner

I was planning to leave the night before my thirteenth birthday. It was on the 8th of August. I'd been 'Rosie Mulligan, the Dumping Ground Kid' for long enough. What I mean to say is that I'm in care. And it's all her fault. Her, as in my horrible step-aunt. She isn't really my step-aunt. It's just that I don't believe that I could be related to such an evil person. Both my parents were really young when they had me. They were both prepared to be good parents and raise me properly but then my mother met another man and they eloped. My father couldn't handle it so he gave me to his sister Rosemary. I was named after her but I changed my name to Rosie.

I am in care because of Rosemary's repulsive daughter Suzanne. I told Rosemary a million times that I didn't break Suzanne's arm or shred her clothes, she did it herself to get me into trouble. She took Suzanne's side of course, and I was booted into care while Miss High and Mighty went on holidays. I wonder does she have a conscience? But what I didn't realise, at the time, was that by putting me into care Step-Aunt Rosemary was doing the nicest thing she'd ever done for me. Because when I went into care, I knew, I just knew that I would be able to get out of there. It'd be so great. I wouldn't have to go to school and I'd get to do whatever I wanted to. It would be the best thing that had ever happened to me in my miserable thirteen years on this planet.

It would be perfect, except for Ciaran. He's a baby that's just come here and I really like him and I'm pretty sure he likes me too. I have a real knack with kids. They stop crying when I hold them; they play with me and I can give them their bottle. I was lying in bed one night in the Dumping Ground when I had an idea. I could take him with me! We could live in the tree house at the end of Mr. Morrissey's field. I'd nick food and blankets and I would raise him like my brother. When he was old enough he could go to school. Of course we'd have changed our names. I wouldn't let him be thick like me. He would go to University and everything. When I was old enough I could get a job and rent a flat for us. I'd made up my mind. We were going to leave the following night. I packed all my clothes into a bag and hid it under my bed. I was going to have to pack

Ciaran's things later, because Shelly, our supervisor, would get suspicious. The night I was going to leave, the night before my birthday, I walked into Ciaran's room and stared down at his little face. What was doing? I couldn't run away with a baby! We wouldn't survive. I leant down and kissed him on his soft cheek. I quickly scribbled a note to Shelly saying that I had left and was going to take Ciaran with me but decided not to. I finished off saying that I was born a loner and would always be a loner.

Iraq 2003

G.I.s are riding
On a great steel horse
And sweeping from the sky
In aluminium cross
Spoiling for a battle
I'm sure they cannot win
Kicking up the dust and
Making awful din.

Chopper hopper Colonels
Commanding many sons
Trigger –happy young men
Careless with their guns
Women running crying
Bleeding from the head
History repeats itself
Caesar is not dead.

They are following orders
Emanating from the Bush
Never looking backward
Just push push push
Slaughtering and bombing
And crumpling as they go
Ask them why they do it
They simply do not know.

Their Generals know better
The rewards are very great
But a lesson will be learned
When it's much too late
The native loves his country
Made of forest, oil or sand
And he'll fight a strong invader
Till the last man stands.

The Tour Guide

I see them, two girls, both pale, one clutching the familiar red of the information leaflet and walking deliberately in the direction of the great house. As I look through the side panel of the door of the ancestral home and see, as every Saturday, the hordes of people milling around the castle five hundred yards away. This site is one of the busiest in Ireland and today it shows it, bursting with foreign students, coach-parties and Americans. Very few come up here to us in the old house, though. Instead, they run over the battlements of the castle, listen to the echoes of their voices in the dungeons and buy sweets from the kiosk. We are overlooked; the also-ran in the guidebook. A shame really, as this is the family seat of the Moriarty's, who bought the land where the castle is and turned some ruins into a fine business. I, Elizabeth and five other employees run the tours of the house with its six rooms open to the public.

Of course, it's the locked rooms that they're really interested in, and who can blame them? I see them crane their necks back as they pass a private bathroom where the door has swung open to reveal a crumpled towel or a pool of condensation.

'It's just like your own,' I yearn to say. But that wouldn't be appropriate as they are the paying customers. Instead I direct them to highlights like the twenty-place-setting dining table, commissioned in Scotland and crafted in oak with walnut inlay.

The two visitors, girls, enter the hallway and appear earnest, interested. They pay Agnes, who sits behind a writing desk, French, nineteenth century, and wait for the tour to begin. Standing upright, I finger my crucifix and glance at my notes. I know most of it by heart, but still get nervous after all these years. To help myself, I underlined anything confusing when I started. The hall clock chimes and I stroke my hair and adjust my skirt. I tell the girls that the next tour is ready to begin in three minutes. I notice everything about them without looking directly at them. Today is very hot and I know they are here partly to escape the sun. The smaller one has sunburn on her shoulder and wears glasses. She smiles a lot and makes agreeable murmurs to her friend who is less talkative, looks around more, and betrays impatience in her twitching feet. They tell me they're from Dublin, and here for two days on a tour. Like most people who end up at the house, they have an interest in the bust of Sir Charles and read the inscription. We all wait, and when no one else comes, I begin.

'It's just the two of you. The final tour of the day', I say and they smile, a bit embarrassed.

They are already five steps up the marble stairs but choose to come back down to the door to look at the family tree where I'm pointing.

'You have to start here,' I tell them. Tracing my finger over the tapestry, I map out the births, marriages and deaths of five generations. Not for the first time I confuse Edwina and Evelyn. Who was sister and who was cousin? I look down at my typed notes and find the relevant underlined information and correct myself. Blushing I leave nothing else out and the girls follow me up to the first floor and the morning room, dining room and billiards room.

My favourite things in the house are the portraits. They speak to me of a bygone age of finery and gentility and they look happy, now retired and mounted on the wall in the family home. Carefully I detail who is who and their relationships to the others. Generations of wives, sisters and daughters beam out at me and I highlight the details that I have noticed over the years, such as a family dog hiding behind a screen in one and an unexplained ring on the finger of another. These people are also my friends. Once I am drowned out as a fan of light falls into the room from the door opposite. It is James with his tour group, the second last of the day. They are laughing and he is joking as he bows in the doorway to usher out three Mediterranean women. My girls notice them too as they sweep down the stairs chattering. I smile but it is too late as his deep voice carries up the stairs as the rest of him descends.

In the Ladies' sitting-room the two girls purr admiration as visitors normally do in the face of twelve-foot windows, marble fireplaces and uninterrupted views of the lawns, topiary and pond. They linger admiring the window seats, bookcases and silverware. I draw them to the family paintings and explain their notable associations. One girl, the taller, wanders off to look at the gun cupboard and I concentrate on her friend. She looks after the taller one who finishes her circuit of the room and comes back to us. The small girl admires the curtains.

'I don't know if they are original,' I say. 'They're in such good repair'. I feel inadequate as my stomach lurches. No one has ever asked me about the curtains before. Nevertheless, she smiles in agreement and I feel she appreciates my words.

I bring them to each remaining room in turn and escort them down the stairs. The taller one shows she is anxious to be off by accelerating off to sign the visitors' book. Agnes opens the heavy door and they pass out into the sunshine outside with murmurs of approval and politeness. I watch them go right down the steps and walk into the centre of the setting sun. Head bowed, I sign the visitors' book in my own name. Agnes has turned to counting the money in the black cashbox and doesn't see. I don't know why I did it. As I cross my 'T' it feels like I'm part of the story of the house, transported in through the yellowing pages of the book. My autograph does not stand out from the other signatures.

There are shadows in some of the rooms now as the day is drawing to a close. The sun has visited each room in turn and is now dying. Twenty past six and I wait in my car at the bottom of the avenue, on my journey home, as the indicator beats for the left turn. I am the last to leave the house as Agnes left a few minutes earlier to catch dinner in town before a play. Her thoughtful little present sits on the back seat. A curl of lavender ribbon sits on top and I imagine what could lie within the box. I see the tourist traffic whiz by on its way west to the beaches, and my eye wanders to the beautiful weeping willow that hangs over the gate. It is unchanged despite all the comings and goings and millions of footsteps to the great house. I knock the car out of gear and step out for a moment. I turn as a noise behind me draws my attention. The groundsman is closing the great iron gates behind me. The house is sealed in silhouette behind them. To me it looks so beautiful in the evening summer light. It is I who is alone as I tip my white envelope into the post box on the wall. I hold onto it for a few seconds and swallow and then let go. It is a simple thank you to the family for all their kindnesses to me over eight years, on this my final day. I get back into the car and make the left turn back to the city and I do not look back.

The Shed.

Old Stanley stove, *high nellie* bicycle,
Plastic flowers still fresh,
Schoolbooks, faded, loosening.
First bicycle, one red welly, satchel.
In fashion, out of fashion.
Shipped out, later painted back in;
A catalogue of memory barely held together.
Second shelf, photo half-hidden, son and father.
A little temple in the gloom,
Left aside this cipher to the past.

Welcome

It's the smell of scented clover
Or a sweet baked apple pie.
It's a cooling breeze in summer
When the temperatures are a bit too high.
It's seeing familiar faces
A handshake and a smile.
It's hearing your favourite music play
When you think you've lost your way.
It's the colour of a burning sunset
Where rests your weary soul.
It's a loving hug of comfort
When you find you're safely home.

The Great Escape

It was a bright crisp day and, as dawn approached, all was quiet. The only sounds were that of the water lapping against the canal walls and gondolas, and the odd call of birds just wakening

Suddenly the tranquil state of sleepy Venice was disturbed by the sudden clatter of feet along the cobbles, followed by the shout of, 'he's vanished, where'd he go?' out of a dark doorway. Behind them slipped a young man, unseen and unheard by the group of men who were evidently searching for him. This man was dressed in black from head to toe and he was wearing, what appeared to be, plimsolls.

The young man was on the most wanted list of convicts, and his name was James Browne...son of Thomas Brown, the most powerful drug lord of all times. Powerful, but small, he had been caught earlier on this year. Tomas had been easy to catch, as his legs were too short to make a fast getaway, apparently. James, however, had proved more difficult. The police nicknamed him Trixie Dixie because somehow he always knew when the police were coming and abandoned his factories...taking all his produce with him.

It seemed as though he was going to escape again. Then James let out an almighty sneeze. In this small back street it sounded like an explosion. The sound ricocheted off every wall, shaking the shutters of the nearby house, echoing round and round, and then stopped as suddenly as it had started. For a split second James was rooted to the spot, frozen in time, until he saw the police simultaneously turn and start running his way. Only then did he come to his senses and hightail it out of there. Clatter, clatter along the cobles they went. Patter, patter he went. Round the corner he went, round the corner they came, and stopped dead in their tracks. Thud, thud, crash, they all banged into each other and fell over.

Picking themselves up off the ground, straightening their jackets and brushing themselves off, they stared open-mouthed and wide-eyed. This back street came to a dead end, but James had disappeared. There were no doorways which he could have entered, so they were completely baffled. 'Ping' a coin hit one of the men on his head. Picking it up he noted that it was foreign, from China to be exact. The police simultaneously looked up, knowing, yet hoping it wasn't so, and sure enough, there stood James on a balcony laughing down at them. Giving a jolly wave he started strolling back the way he had come, hopping from balcony to balcony. The police followed his progress on the ground, until James had run out of balconies on that level. There was a steep climb up to the next balcony, and no doubt James would have attempted and succeeded in reaching the next level, except that there was nothing to hold on to, so James dived into the canal and disappeared.

He was underwater and swimming quickly. He reached the outer-most gate and swam underneath. On the other side, the police heard an outboard motor kick into life. By now they were too exhausted to go after him; they knew they wouldn't catch him anyway...this story was all over The News.

A year later they are still after him. They went to China and found his factory deserted. Then they went to India and found evidence he'd been there but they were too late.

Now I hear they are somewhere in Australia hunting for him. James Browne is taking them for a ride. I don't think they will catch him, well not anytime this year, at least!

Eagle

I am eagle proud and free,
Flying way up high,
I fly on silent wings,
In the whisper of the wind,
My eyes ever searching, never miss a thing,
I am quiet yet sometimes I am loud.

My flight is enchanting, as I dip and soar and circle,
Like a dance rehearsed,
To the eye I am pleasing,
But watch, as I land silent as a breath,
Upon my unsuspecting prey,

I am deadly as a vice,
But approach me not for I shall flee,
And never shall you see me again,
For I, am wild and free,
And fly with the wind!

Life Goes On
Trilogy of an old man

This is dedicated to my granddad

Poem a haon

He stands there
Strong, tall
Smiles as he sees his life.
Hard times, happy times
Now he is ready, knowing he is right.

She looks at him eyes telling nothing
Love is so hard and thin.
Cannot make her mind up to tell him yes or no
His hair red like fire
His hands strong to hold her, to keep her safe.

His heart breaks.
She moves from his fingers
And fades into the shadows.

Poem a dó

An elderly man is crying
Looking at the coffin
Where his heart lies
His face all tense and he questioned
Why not him?
Can he go tonight!
His head looks up – eyes wet
Blue piercing through
Her voice echoes
He smiles – looks over
An elderly man is crying.

<u>Poem a trí</u>

Looking at this picture
I held her close
Loved her since I can remember
Her hair flowing down her back
Mingling with my fingers
She looks at me
Smiles
Her eyes twinkle as lights
Calling me home
Her hands on my shoulders
As they played our song.

Perseverance

Once more to our Sisyphean task:
Thrice our goal we sought
And thrice were we denied.
One hill we conquered but at
Another faltered.
So we begin again with vigour fresh.
Prevail we must at length
Or beseech the gods to let us
Choose another hill.

The Dream Council

It all started at the beginning of time. Back then people didn't have dreams, so they were cranky and bored because they didn't have anything to dream about. So God invented the Dream Council. He invented it because his people were so cranky they didn't pray anymore, so he was bored. The Head of the Dream Council (really she was just a head. Her husband King Alexander of Alexandria beheaded her for eating his slice of apple tart. That just shows how cranky he was.) The Head's name was Beatrice but she'd changed it to Miss Sara. Second to the Head were the Arrangers. Each Arranger had a topic such as Composers, Inventors, Mechanics etc. Then each Arranger had to give ordinary people ideas about their topic. For example: Charlie Smith Topic #265, Inventors, would give someone an idea for an invention. Then that person might become an inventor so Charlie would put a tick on his list of successful dreams. And whoever had the most successful dreams at the end of the year would become Dream Councillor of the year.

Last year Dr. Frank Jones won with #311 successful dreams. His topic was careers. Everyone always said he got the easiest topic but Miss Sara would not change topics. Once you get your topic it's your topic forever. This year, however, was group year and the councillors were too busy deciding what symphony to give Beethoven; too busy to notice a small child enter the room. The girl was a very ragged creature but still quite pretty. She slowly and very quietly crept up to Miss Sara, who was arguing with Councillor Donald Brickell about what not to put into Beethoven's second last bar of his symphony. The child was so quiet that when she tapped Miss Sara's shoulder, (she wore a prosthetic body to look more important) Miss Sara jumped a mile.

'What the! ...' cried Miss Sara after she had landed back in her chair. Dr. Jones came up behind Miss Sara.

'Hello love,' he whispered. 'What are you doing here?'

'That's exactly what I'd like to know!' shouted Miss Sara.

'I'm here to see M ... Miss S ... Sara,' stuttered the little girl. She was so small and frail looking that she was shivering with fear.

33

'Well, that's me. So what do you want?' asked Miss Sara harshly.

'Don't be so hard on the poor child,' said Donald Brickell.

'What's your name, hon?' Frank asked the little girl.

'I'm El … El … Elizabeth O' Grady' she stammered. 'I'm here to ask a favour.' The Councillors had sat Elizabeth down because she was shaking so badly. They found out that she was seven years old and lived in a run-down little house in Dublin. She wanted to give her father a dream. A dream that would restore his faith in his business. Her father, Pat O' Grady, was a carpenter. He had worked very hard in his workshop for ten years. He had made beautiful tables, chairs, cupboards and wardrobes but no one wanted to buy his work. He lost faith in his business, in his work and in himself. Elizabeth wanted her father to be happy again. The councillors decided to send Beethoven the unfinished piece and to help Elizabeth. As time wore on, Elizabeth's father began to drink. He spent every penny they had. When he came home each night he would reek of alcohol. Elizabeth hated to see her father like this and would cry herself to sleep each night. Once her father drank so much he missed two days of work. This was very hard on the family. There were six O' Grady children including Elizabeth. For those two days they all went hungry. Their mother, Cáit, was heart-broken watching her little darlings starve. As soon as Pat was ready to go back to work, Cáit went looking for a job. She thought she might get a job as a cook. She did get a job, but not as a cook, as a maid. One day when Elizabeth's mother went out to work, Elizabeth went to Henry Street and went into the third house on the left. This was how she first got into the room. She climbed the stairs to the upper room and went in. The councillors were in there with many books in front of them. They all looked up as she walked in. A few of them smiled but most of them just carried on looking through the books before them. Dr. Jones ushered her towards the top of the room. As she sat down, she sank until you could just see the top of her head over the table. Miss Sara stood up and began to speak.

'Last week Elizabeth O' Grady asked us to give her father a dream, a dream to restore his faith in his business. After much thought, we have decided that there is nothing more important to a man than his family and their welfare. Elizabeth has told us that her father regularly goes to a public house and spends his weekly wages on alcohol' She paused to look down at Elizabeth, who was rapidly sinking even further into her chair, and smiled.

'We have decided,' she continued, 'to give him a nightmare. In this nightmare, he will see himself, three years earlier, working cheerfully in his workshop. Following that, he will see himself as he is today. He will see a drunk, a wastrel and a failure. He will see his family three years ago, happy and carefree. Then he will see them as they are today – starving, worn out and dreading tomorrow. He will see customers coming into his shop, smiling and chatting. He will, finally, see himself sitting in his shop, drunk, with his family all around him, looking disgustedly at him. Hopefully, this will make him see sense.' Miss Sara nodded at all the councillors and sat down. They talked for a few more minutes about when they were going to give Pat the nightmare.

They decided on Wednesday night. Elizabeth had been looking for signs in her father's actions to see if he was reforming himself, but to no avail. On Wednesday night she waited up until her father came home. She heard him fall asleep immediately as soon as he had gotten into bed. It was some time later before Elizabeth fell asleep. The next morning Elizabeth heard sounds in the kitchen. She crept downstairs and found, to her delight, that her father was in there singing! She ran towards him and gave him a huge hug. He picked her up, swung her round and called her his 'little buttercup'. He then went off to work. Elizabeth raced to Henry Street and up to the third house on the left. She hurried up the stairs and burst into the room. She hugged all the councillors and even Miss Sara! Elizabeth was ecstatic with the results of the nightmare. She, finally, had the happy, sober father she had missed so badly.

Reel Life.

We met long ago,
Faces flirted across a table.
Time dims, memories fade.
Face appearing on a screen,
Seeming unrelated,
Super nova explodes,
Conclusion is confusion.

Tracing Memories.

My mind is a dusty room
Of memories
Till one image draws all together.

The Lighter Side of the Mayo Train

Once again I stand at the station, glancing at my watch. 14:53! After months of travelling to and from Dublin and Castlebar, I no longer worried when the 14:47 came and went, and no hint of a train in sight. I calmly watched the *new ones* and the *hard of learning* who impatiently pace the platform, craning their necks to see the first glimpse of the train. I learnt from experience that I would hear the whistle blow shortly before it arrived; therefore I no longer strain my neck for no reason.

I watch the train gliding around the corner and calmly walk to the wall where I have left my little bag. In Castlebar the chance of someone nicking your bag is as possible as winning the lotto (no disrespect intended to the players.)

The new ones rush to get through the door, cramming to get a seat, although at this stage of the journey, the percentage is about 10 to 1 for any person looking for a place to rest their weary weekend bones. Without much ado I settle in my seat, dig out my crisps, book, magazine, mobile, ciggies and any other luxury I might need for my four-hour journey, and sit back to relax for a nice quiet ride through the *green jewel* of Ireland. But alas! That is not to be. Next stop Manulla Station.

I glance up, disturbed by the horrific noise and am faced with an enemy-advance of a gaggle of seniors returning from a weekend in the country. This is not bad, you say. Have you ever been overrun in a confined space by people with various degrees of deafness? (Now all the seniors must probably think: just you wait till you get older.)

Once I start getting used to the raised volume of cackling, I notice the degree of competition. Each candidate competes for the highest points of sympathy. One seems to be gaining on points. Her deafness, selective I might add, outweighs her lack of sight, which she demonstrates by bringing the train ticket so close to her nose that she leaves smudges of lipstick on the edge of the ticket. She then tops this by spilling scalding coffee all over the floor, conveniently missing her foot. I suppose there is a limit to sympathy. One doesn't really want to experience actual pain. A bevy of helpers fuss over her

37

after responding to her fourth or sixth wail of despair. At this stage, I am having great difficulty controlling my giggle for fear of being branded a psychopath by her helpers. I mentally pass her a medal and give her the highest score.

I settle back to my book. People come and go and soon the seniors have competition crowding into the carriage. They are the Super Troopers consisting of five to seven young people all aged between sixteen and twenty. They struggle towards their seats, weighed down by a month's supply of Bulmers or something similar, counter weighed by fags and portable CD players. The noise gets out of hand. The contest is in full swing – varying between one group exchanging degrees of *lockedness* and the other groups snide sniggering, whispered remarks about the youth of today, which by some miracle can be heard clearly by 90% of the group. Did I mention selective hearing?

Who needs a book or magazine on the train? The Dublin to Westport line includes entertainment, although it is not mentioned on the ticket; it comes free of charge.

The fare of course also comes with a live fashion show. All types of slim to not-so-slim prance past the seat, displaying the latest ranges of trainers, hipsters, belly piercing and belly-rings (nothing to do with metal objects.) Soon the convoy of snackers passes you in a drunken, swaying motion, and not all due to the train. They return heavily laden back to their allocated places, to resume their previous doings. Some in higher spirits than others.

By now you might think the entertainment has come to an end. No way. As it is said: the show is not over till the fat lady sings, in this case it's group no. 2, the non-deaf ones – but alas, you envy the seniors now!

Inheritance

A Viking Longboat sailed yesterday
toward Dublin harbour.
With only a seagull's timeless cry,
waters parted.
She had no shadow.

It's all contained here, a single jewel
under torn concrete, a harsh cry in silence,
lap of waves and still reflections.
The moon had dimmed, swooping low
across the water. Out of the clouds,
a sea dragon roared and plunged with grace.
Suddenly, something
that could have been more than a myth.

Poetry left us on such plunging ships,
to return so familiar we never recognised
that we fought once to deny we ever wanted it.
Watching the sun burn away its shroud of fog,
it's easy to deny moments of knowing nothing,
and seeing everything.

Dreams belong entirely to unconscious minds
that see beyond barriers, back
to where changes began so suddenly.
We built cities on them.

Evening Sun on Sea

The sun is glowing orange,
Perfectly contained in pewter sky.

Casts its softening light
on your rippling silver as it descends
between the island and the cliff face.

Reaching to enfold
your mercurial blanket that flows
in soothing rhythm, moving and calming
to carry with assured ease to peace.

The Front

We could have been mates
sharing jokes, relaxing at The Inn.
Discussing girls, cars and
what the future brings.

Yet here we stand, face to face,
barrel to barrel, confusion to fear.
Our eyes locked, emotions echoed.
What now? Our worlds disappear.

I can smell the fear
rising from his uniform.
A battle-scarred image of myself.
We were taught to fight, but no lessons on death.

Staring eyes locked on uncertainty,
trembling hands gripped for survival.
Legs that refuse to run.
His eyes blink, his finger tenses.

I pull the trigger and my youth dies with him.
I am old.

Extract from a novel: Breaking the Shadow.

The sun glares upon the salty sidewalk, angrily heating the stones, so that blisters will form on those who tread barefoot. The rhythm of its African anger seeped into the open window. She could start the ignition and move away, but it would follow her anyway. She is forced to sit there and think about her sins.   A face materialises through the hazy air, she can see those eyes, very intent now, very piercing. Out of habit she climbs over to the passenger side so Torben can do the driving.

'It's ok' he says walking around the car. 'You drive. I'll do the talking' He wanted to be alone with her, away from the influences of friends and enemies.

The sun stares again, stretching itself with satisfaction over the dashboard Torben tries to smile, but his expression is closed.

'Are you really sure this is what you want?' he asks.
She has rehearsed her reply often, yet she mumbles something else.

'I'm terribly sorry, is there any way I can get you through this?' If only she had persuasive powers. But she has no natural graces, no cajoling ways.

Her body is hot all over, yet she feels cold inside. Torben turns his head and she can see the pudgy profile against the shimmering heat. He looks down at her hands and she has to strain to hear.

'Yes, I see.' He sighs and puts his hands on hers. 'You always wanted more than I could give...you love him...don't you?'

'I don't know yet – I think I do.' She feels as if she's on the rebound but she dare not let him know. She should have kept quiet but it's like talking to an old friend. So she tells him what she sees in Frank and then realising her mistake, she stops talking in mid sentence. The silence stretches for a few minutes, maybe more, and then she can't help herself and leaning towards him, she lets herself be lost in his warm and familiar smell.   Suddenly a voice behind them breaks the awkwardness.

'Hey, what's this soppy stuff, are you two back together again?' She struggles to free herself from his embrace and greet Torben's brother.

'Things have changed John.' What a stupid thing to say, so obvious, so unconvincing, but she leaves it at that.

The afternoon passed quickly and without incident. Laughter came easily and she found herself at ease. They discussed past and present situations and at some stage they both forgot that John was there. Although he never seemed to mind. She could read no animosity in Torben's eyes, but it was obvious even in his confused state of anxiety that he was waiting for something, hanging on to a thread of what they used to be.

And that's when it dawned on her. A vision. A thrill of fear ran up her spine, and changed her mood. Used to it, Torben never noticed. She was relieved when they finally left. She wanted time to think of this, her vision. It felt real. As if it had already come to pass. She did not let go of that thought for several hours as it tossed and turned her bed sheets that night. Finally she made peace with the idea, and decided to make the necessary arrangements in the morning.

Fairytales

I was a changeling child,
twisted into life,
from warm straw and frozen dewdrops.
The child in my cot, replaced
in darkness, carried carefully
to the world beyond, of moving objects,
cursed stillness in moonlit trees.
The old people warned it could happen,
and saw through me ever since.

Trying to understand their faces,
smiles that could hold you tight or swallow you whole.
(Nothing like childhood nightmares and facetious neighbours,
'Couldn't you just eat her up?')

A man I met last week reminded me of this,
talking to himself in foreign words for a good
ten minutes before I realised he was addressing me.
I was staring in a mirror wearing headphones so that
his words, the song lyrics and the secret language
with which I must address myself
mingled together and drifted away.

I remembered another life where I changed
beyond recognition, moving figures
shaped into their destiny by nature's forces
steering us, wrapped in our words,
histories and nameless faces
in barely remembered dreams; a life
where people grieved for what they never understood,
and survival was an alternative
to becoming a substance rather than a solid.
I remembered a summer evening,
when proud parents left the nursery window open.
Well…

Rough Justice

Scene 1 – Int. – Garda Station – Night

We are in the locker room of a garda station where there is a young
female garda putting on a belt with a radio and baton attached.
Beside her is an older male garda tucking his shirt into his trousers
over a large belly.

Frank
So this is your first night on patrol then?

Sinead
Yes, anything I should know?

Frank
Ah, musha not really. Tis a pity it's a Saturday, we could've broke
you in easy otherwise, but sure you'll be grand.

He puts on a jumper and she puts on a high visibility jacket.

Frank
We'll go easy tonight. All set then?

She nods and they exit.

Scene 2 – Int. – Pub – Night

A group of men stand around holding pints. One man is the centre of
attention, as he animatedly tells a story while spilling his pint.

Sean
So there I am, pissed as a fart, and I've missed the turn three times.

He takes a long slug from his pint.

                    Sean
So I'm damned if I'm going round the friggin roundabout again
                    right?

The other men nod at this urging him to continue.

                    Sean
              So I said I'd reverse.

Scene 3 – Int. – Garda van – Night

Frank is driving. Sinead looks bored as she stares out the van
window.

                    Frank
              Oh here we go.

Sinead looks up eagerly.

                    Frank
Sure we may as well take this lad in and save ourselves the bother
                    later.

They pull up and beside the van sitting on the ground is a homeless
Sean with a bottle of Buckfast and a cup on the ground.

                 Homeless Man
Ah for fucks sake, can a man not have a drink in peace these days.

                    Frank
Come on now Christy, you know you shouldn't be drinking that in
                    public.

He handcuffs the Christy and after some mumbling and grunting
from him, he manages to put him in the back of the van.

                    Sinead

                     46

Do you know him?

Frank

Ha I do, and after a few nights you'll know them all yourself too.

He walks back to the driver's door of the van, laughing to himself. Sinead, after some time looking at the spot where Christy had been sitting, reaches down and picks up the plastic cup of coppers. She then goes to the passenger seat of the van.

Scene 4 – Int Pub – Night

We are back at the same crowd of people. They all now have shots in their hands.

Man 1
1,2,3

They all knock back the shots. One man winces and then pushes his way through the crowd. They all laugh at him.

Man 2
That poor fuckers an awful lightweight!!

Man 1
Go on anyway Sean.

Sean

Right ya, so I'm fucked you know, here I am looking in the rear view mirror, (Takes another slug from a now fresh pint) And I'm watching the guard suss things out with the eejit I backed into. (Another gulp of pint) Next thing he's walking towards me. Now he's at the window, and I roll it down. 'Howya Guard' I says. Is there much damage? (He's smiling and all the other men are looking on in anticipation)Do you know what he says to me then? 'Ara go on ahead there you, your man behind is so drunk he thinks you were reversing on the roundabout!

Man 2
Ah you're joking?

Sean
Am I shite, I swear to you now that's what the poor fucker said to
me.

He takes another drink. Someone bangs into him and the pint spills
everywhere.

Sean (Turning around)
You'd want to watch where you're going buddy.

Man 3 (Looking worriedly to the others)
Come on Sean leave it.

Scene 5 – Int. – garda van – Night

Sinead and Frank are in the van. Frank is again driving. Sinead is
biting her nails.

Frank
Ah sure we're doing them a favour really, the poor ol'eejits, ya know
giving them a place to stay for the night and all.

Sinead
Mmmm

Frank looks towards her confused, and a little insulted.

Scene 6 – Int – Pub – Night

A brawl has now broken out in the pub, in which Sean is in the
middle of.

Sean
Stupid bloody foreigner, can't ya watch where your flippin going.

Bouncer (Holding Sean under the arms)
Come on you, out with ya.

He drags him away and throws him out of the pub.

Scene 7 – Ext - pub - Night

Sean is on the ground, on a road outside the pub. He stands up and from behind him we see two bright lights, there is the sound of wheels braking and a horn blowing, Sean stands bewildered. The vehicle stops and out steps Sinead and Frank.

Frank
Jesus, you could have been bloody killed, what are ya doing standing in the middle of the road.

Sean just looks at the two Guards, from one to the other, and then vomits all over Sinead.

Sinead (Disgusted)
Oh Jesus, oh gross.

Frank
Ah for feics sake. Give us your handcuffs Sinead.

Sinead
Aw god, this is disgusting, here ya go.

She hands him the handcuffs.

Frank (handcuffing Sean)
No one said it would be glamorous.

Sean

Let go of me, you've no right to do this to me. I have rights you
know, I'll sue ye.

Frank

You're under arrest from being drunk and disorderly and possibly
causing an accident therefore being a menace to society. (To Sinead)
Take off that jacket and put it in the back with this yoke, let him put
up with the smell.

They both go to the back of the van. Frank throws Sean into the back
of the van and Sineád throws in her jacket. Frank closes one of the
doors and behind it is a man. He is unshaven and dirty and resembles
a homeless man. He begins to laugh hysterically at the sight of
Frank.

Frank

Jaysus, will this night ever end.

Man

Oh ho ho ho, tis yourself garda. Well I'd take off me hat to ya if I
had one. A he he he. Any chance of the loan of a tenner Guard. (He
stumbles drunkenly) Woah there matey. Ha ha like a pirate ooh arr.
(He now has his face right up against Franks) Ooh arr ooh arr, here
give us that baton there it can be me fishing rod he he he he.

He attempts to take the baton from around Frank's waist. There are a
couple of people smoking outside the pub, laughing at the situation.
Franks face turns red.

Frank (Grabbing the man)

Right in you go too.

Sinead

Sir, we don't have any more handcuffs.

Frank

I couldn't give a shite, he's coming with us anyway.

50

He puts the man in the back of the van, closes both doors, they both return to the front of the van, get in and drive off.

Scene 8 – Ext – Garda Station – Night.

The van pulls up outside the door. Sinead and frank go to the back and open the doors.

Frank

Here we'll take Christy first and let them too eejits sit there annoying each other.

Sinead goes into the van and emerges with Christy in toe. Frank closes the van doors, locks it and they all go inside.

Scene 9 – Int. Garda van – Night

Sean is slumped against the van with his hands cuffed behind his back. The van is sitting cross-legged.

Man

Well sonny boy, did ya ever meet a pirate before??

Sean

Ah fuck off ya loon.

Man

I take it you haven't then, you'd know to play nice if ya had my boy. (He gets up, goes to Sean and puts his arms around him) Us pirates you see are a force to be reckoned with.

Sean

Get off me ya physco! Help! Someone help!

The mans hands come back into view and in them is Sean's wallet.

51

Man
It's alright my boy, you're not my type. I'll just take this thanks.

Sean
Gimme that back you weirdo, do ya not realize where we are!

Man (sitting back down)
I Know where we are alright, a he he he.

The doors of the van open and Sinead and Frank are there. Frank goes into the van and takes Sean by the arm, escorting him out of the van.

Sean
Hey I've been assaulted, by that pirate there, I mean your man, he took my…

Frank
Oh I'm sure ya have. Come on now, a bit of cop-on out of you and you'll be out in the morning.

Sean
But I…(Trails off with his head down)

Frank (to Sinead)
There was a time ya know when the Guards in this country got a little bit of respect.

Resurrection 5.30 a.m. Summertime

(Recovery and re-discovery using imagery of a ship being brought
back from the bottom of the sea.)

Creaking, straining against the comfort of the sea bed
The newly revealed silt will feel the emptiness
Of the ever-flowing sea water
Which has rotted and claimed
The wreck of the ship
Almost as its own.
But not yet!
For it is moving upwards.
I see
Myself
Flexing the old muscles
And responding
Ignoring pain, for need of movement is immediate.
Don't let me ask 'can I bear this?' – there's no going back.
At last I am away in unnatural seeming flight.
Light grows in the distance.
Blue newness seems bright to the eye and welcome
Like an old friend.
I stand
To see
The sun rising slowly again.
I hear the dawn-chorus; see the quickness of bird-flight;
Content to be alone, peace like still water in my soul,
And then to be aware
Of a burgeoning growth of greenness
Here and everywhere for miles.
I watch everything in the cool of quiet sunrise,
(Everyone's asleep)
And give silent thanks.

Anger

If there was no anger
There would be no need
For borders, fences, lines on maps.
The Whitethorn tree stands fast,
Spreading wide it's roots
Threading through the soil
Grasping with finger-like greed
Through the ditches for it's earthly goods,
Clutching unworthily
At damp soil.
The untidiness of the hills and fields
Is as familiar to the eye
As the toast crumbs on the cosy kitchen table
Where the men are having a hot lunch,
They make declarations about the endless war,
But 'the craic' dissipates any shreds of that anger.
But anger is crouching at somebody else's door, somewhere.

Swamped

You're up there
But you are really down here.
I've seen you cringe at yourself
But I won't be the sharp one anymore,
So that you can call me the
Rough-edged diamond.
I'll push your loud rubbish away
With one finger touch.
One word
And you'll remember who I am.
A mere question:
'Were you saying something to me?'
Reminds you now:
I'm here too.

Another World

William entered his study wearily. He poured himself his usual glass of brandy and was just ready to sit down when he noticed the envelope with his name on it. Lowering himself in to his comfortable armchair, he opened the letter and began to read.

Dear William,

By the time you read this I will be gone. I will be departed from this horrible, cold world. I hope to be in a better place, anywhere is better than here. I know you will find it hard to understand but I can't go on anymore. I don't feel anything for anyone now, but once I felt. I felt love, joy, anger, amusement, happiness and contentment.

My life stopped that night four months ago when I lost my daughters forever. I, too, died that night. The night when that monster broke into our home. I sensed evil, his eyes were dead. I can't sleep without reliving that nightmare he created. I hear the crash of the front door being kicked in and the heavy footsteps on the stairs. Then I smell his putrid breath as he leans over me and ties me tightly to the bed. I looked into his wild eyes and saw all that lurked there was bad and evil. As he ransacked the room taking whatever jewellery he could find, I just wanted him gone. He took everything he could lay his hands on but that wasn't enough.

I can still feel my helplessness as my two little girls came through the door of the bedroom. They started to scream and then he turned and just shot them. My four-year-old girls didn't deserve to die but there was nothing I could do to save them. I couldn't protect them. It was too late. I was powerless. All that blood. I couldn't even hug the girls one last time. I cleaned and cleaned but still all I can see are Daisy and May on the ground in a pool of blood. I want to be with them. It makes no difference that the police caught him the next day. It brings me no comfort to know that he is locked up in prison. That night he made my life a prison.

People tell me that life goes on; well for me it doesn't. The happiest years of my life were spent with the girls. Four delightful, happy years spent playing in the meadow and going for walks in the park. Everyday bought something new and exciting. I used to have reason to smile every morning now I don't have reason to do anything. I can feel the same pain that I feel mirrored in your eyes. The anguish, helplessness, hurt and bewilderment. I know you're hurting too and I wish I could help you. I know you'll understand why I have to do this, and trust that you won't stop me. I hope you'll forgive me and that we'll meet again in a happier place.

I'll love you always,

Amy xxx

William put down the brandy and trudged upstairs to his room. Amy lay on the bed motionless and at peace. There was a smile on her beautiful face again. Lying down beside her on the bed, he reached under it and took out a brown jar. One by one he started to take the little tablets he had been given by his doctor for his depression. As he drifted away from this world he heard Daisy and May call to him.

'Daddy we knew you'd come. We've been waiting for you.' Scooping one child up in each arm he walked towards the light to meet Amy once again.

Two days later a neighbour called in to check on Amy and there she found husband and wife lying side by side, finally at peace.

Stranger

I do not know you,
Do not recognize you,
Yet you say I do.
You say your name, and insist I know you,
But that I don't recall at all.
You say another name,
Female this time,
You say it with such passion, and warmth.
Who is this woman you call,
You must have loved her so!
Tom you say you are,
It sounds familiar, but Tom I do not see.
All I see is you, a stranger, an elderly man crying.
Your eyes red rimmed,
Look up, and I see warmth residing in those depths.
Now you reach to me,
And I back up.
Mary it's me you whisper, I back up even more.
No you must be mistaken; I don't know you at all!

Dad

And then you passed;
Out of this world forever and
Into the next one,
Forever.

Leaving in your wake, now
With your perpetual, eternal sleep,
A wife, two boys, two girls.
A space that is empty, endless
And large.

Fruits of The Celtic Tiger

I leave aside my wish list,
I'm thankful for my health.
I'll never fill my wish list,
I haven't got the wealth.

But hey, who cares?
I've got my friends.
And lots of memories, too.
And chasing up my wish-list
Would spoil a life or two.

My acquaintances are grabbers,
They never have enough.
They've lots in store
And still want more,
While others have it rough

No sense now in talking,
Capitalists expand.
A wheeling and a-dealing
They buy up all the land.
Take pride in their expansion
And spending of their 'grands.'

A Great Honour.

The routine was always the same. The lads, dressed in black jackets, polo-necks and overalls observed the city – Dinny from the front seat, Frankie from behind him. They sat quietly concentrating on the scanners, listening for information on the Brits. Oncoming headlamps shyly illuminated the foggy winter night. I just kept driving steadily along, avoiding known areas of surveillance. Dinny said very little and, as was the custom, wasn't asked. When he felt I was unsure, he'd say *next left* or *next right* as was appropriate – he always knew the way.

Frankie sat silently in the back as I pointed the terracotta coloured Ford along the narrow streets towards the east of the city. We always headed east, that's where most of the work was done.

Dinny was supposedly a shuttering subbie who hired-out a lot of boys to the big sites in and around Belfast. He was respected and feared as a veteran hitman – he was not one to mess with. Dinny was high on the RUC list of wanted and had dodged them frequently, usually shielding himself with indiscriminate gunfire from a Kalashnikov or an Uzi. The trail of casualties was an embarrassment to the leadership, but they never reprimanded him. He knew too much to be disciplined. He was rarely on the building sites himself, spending most of his time *pricing jobs* – most likely surveillance or other duties. A lot of money was washed through the building industry and Dinny was doing well, with his men involved in several projects. It was rumoured he'd bought a farm in Co. Clare and had a couple of houses in Dundalk. But no one would ask for confirmation.

Frankie was a plasterer by trade, sometimes working down in Dublin, other times up here. Like the rest of us, he rarely spoke when Dinny was in the company, but was quite chatty otherwise. He usually talked football, commented on women he'd noticed or been with in the past, and enjoyed darts. Like most of us, he drank in one of the clubs on the Falls at weekends, but didn't drink during the week.

Frankie's two brothers had died outside a bookies one evening a few years previously. His sister was now a widow, thanks

60

to a Loyalist bullet in the back of her husband's head.   Frankie became more involved after his best friend was killed along with his girlfriend in a chip shop the previous Christmas twelve months.

In the army, Frankie's speciality was domestic hits. He had a failure rate of zero. Best in the business. Professionalism born out of vengeance, people said. Frankie was sometimes referred to as the *Widowmaker In Chief* – a title he hated. He took no pride in his efforts, just care and attention. He never discussed operations and was very cool, almost relaxed on jobs.

'Down here,' Dinny snapped. His voice had changed. It was more direct, more focused. I knew we were getting nearer. My stomach tightened.

'Left,' he said as we approached a roundabout. He rarely moved his head but his eyes rolled all the time, watching, looking, observing. He surveyed the rows of council houses while I kept driving. The silence was punctuated by random bursts of speech through the white noise, as taxi drivers, lorry drivers and kids with CB radios provided invaluable information on checkpoints, troop movements and small-time riots. Sometimes I wished that Dinny or Frankie'd say that they'd spotted cover – some of our own – or that they'd noticed emergency getaway transport placed strategically –but never a word. Nothing was said because nothing was seen – we were on our own.

Dinny took the balaclava from his pocket, a sure sign that we were getting nearer our target. When he pulled it over his head, we were less than a hundred yards away.

'That's it, sixteen.' Dinny's voice distorted by synthetic fibre and genuine tension. I stopped the car on the road outside the house and switched off the motor, following instructions just like I had done on six previous jobs. Frankie opened the back door, his balaclava already on as he stepped into the night air. I waited in the car, watching them run to the door, and keeping an eye on the area.

Number sixteen was a brown brick-faced council house with white windows and black concrete roof tiles, like so many more in the city. Inside a family were probably having their supper. For some poor bastard, probably my own age, it would be the last supper. He'd have a pretty wife and two children. Protestants didn't have as many children as Catholics. If he were one of us, he'd have four or maybe five. There would be a wedding photograph on top of the telly in a golden fame made in Hong Kong, her in her white dress, fanned out at the bottom, on the right of the picture: he'd be in a dark suit, proudly displaying a white carnation. They'd probably use that picture on The News tomorrow.

There wouldn't be much conversation at the table, they'd be hungry, it would be a functional, rather than social meal. Spaghetti Bolognaise or maybe chops and chips. The kids would be mannerly, a boy and a girl. The girl would probably be the eldest, maybe eight or nine. The boy, a respectable two years younger. The father'd be a welder or a fitter or maybe a forklift-driver. Probably be in the shipyard or Shortts. His biggest crime wasn't a crime at all. We simply knew his address. He was probably spotted going in to a UDA meeting, or seen talking in public to someone in the Association. It didn't matter. We could have gone next door – to number fourteen or eighteen or eighty or anywhere else in the estate. They were all the same here. *Legitimate targets.*

I wondered how I could get out. Head south? I often considered it. They'd find me though, the cells are everywhere. The fate of deserters was often recalled at training camps, outside Mass and in the pubs. Kneecapping I'd tolerate, but they'd probably finish me off.

Fuck it anyway.

The front door offered little resistance to Frankie's right foot. The swift forward thrust was powerful and precise. He had his gun ready, held firmly in his right hand as he stepped aside to let Dinny – the senior man – in first. Dinny didn't do doors, preferring trigger work instead. They both disappeared inside and through the open car window and the smashed front door, I could hear the shrieks.

'No, not in front of the kids,' she screamed. She didn't even swear. Not a fuck to be heard. Polite – the Prods. Even in the hysteria that followed, a fuck wasn't to be heard. Amazing that. Very polite.

Dinny came out first, running towards the car. Frankie followed, slower – his bigger frame didn't travel as swiftly. I started up the engine.

'Get to fuck outahere,' Dinny shouted. As he scrambled into the car something moved behind us to the left. I turned and through the side window I saw someone running from behind number twelve. Too late. I saw the instantaneous flash. Frankie stumbled. Oh Fuck! He went down. The big man slumped limply, facing us, eyes staring from the driveway – a desperate look of helplessness; of expectation. I looked at Dinny.

'Getthefuckaway,' Dinny shouted again.

'Frankie's hit,' I shouted back.

'Fuck Frankie. Get on the road or we'll all be killed.'

'We can't leave him, he'll finish him.' The gunman fired again.

Dinny pointed the gun in the direction of the hitman and squeezed the trigger. The snap of the firing-pin brought an immediate result. Dinny was a great triggerman. Experience counts when they're firing too.

'What are you waiting for?' Dinny's eyes were glazed-over with rage.

Our comrade wasn't moving though his stare was perfectly focused. I thought of having to break the news to Frankie's wife. I felt a sudden urge to puke.

The women always knew what was going on, but they never said anything and never, ever, asked any questions – never anything to implicate them. Nothing to deny denial.

'We can't just leave him,' I said. Dinny glanced at our injured colleague and spat his frustration.

'This is the last fucking time I'm going on a job with a sissy like you. Will you get this fucking motor away down the road or we'll all be dead.'

'You fucking drive it so,' I said as I started to open the door.

'No,' he snapped, 'Wait here. I'll go. Cover me. Get your weapon and don't desert your fucking post.' As he left the car I took the pistol from my jacket pocket and released the catch.

Dinny knelt beside Frankie, and seemed to whisper something. Then bending down he made the sign of the Cross on the injured man's forehead and putting the tip of the barrel firmly against Frankie's temple, squeezed the trigger.

I didn't hear the click. The head jerked and a spurt of something dark splattered Dinny's arm.

He'd fucking shot Frankie.

I watched him turn around, to check for any more armed Prods. This was my chance. I pointed the gun at the back of his head and waited. When he turned and faced me, I squeezed the trigger and in an instant he was on the ground.

'There you bastard. That'll teach you.' I'd got him in the centre of the forehead. All the evenings and weekends in the training camps finally paid dividends. Dinny was on the ground beside Frankie. My first hit.

*****

The following evening, comrades from the fifth battalion ushered the hundreds of people in, and later out of the council house for the removal of Frankie's remains. The mourners closely observed the Brits whose armoured vehicles were positioned at both ends of the street. The Brits watched us closely too, their camouflage protecting their identities behind the glass screens and razor wire. A cacophony of whispers uttered vengeance.

'It's always the good ones,' someone said.

Pity it takes a Protestant bullet to make a Catholic from West Belfast into a *good one.* Or maybe a Catholic bullet – that'd do it too.

'The under-sixteens are forming a guard of honour at Dinny's funeral tomorrow,' a voice behind me whispered. 'He worked so hard for the GAA – they'll miss him a lot.' I could visualise the white armbands made from bed linen, with black crosses drawn with permanent marker. *Dinny – a good one?* A good one for killing a Protestant. They don't know he killed a Catholic too. And that I killed another. The commander signalled me to the front of the queue, and I went into the house.

'I can't believe he was involved in any of that, my Frankie,' Brenda said as she accepted the condolences of neighbours. 'He was a good man. A great father and husband. I can't believe it.'

The black eyeliner made her Labrador eyes even more remarkable, her firm cheekbones and perfect nose. She was the centre of attention; all the volunteers wanted her to know how sorry they were. The boys, seven year old Eamonn and Noel, a year his junior, were smiling. They were proud of their dad, ignorant of what had happened, already sworn to revenge, a revenge to be carried out on the Prods.

After the prayers, Frankie's boys unfolded a tricolour from a rectangular cardboard box and placed it on top of the sealed coffin. Their mother embraced her sons as tears streamed down the faces of all three.

As I stood outside on the roadside I felt a gentle tap on my right arm. Steely, piercing eyes met mine. The solemn grey face of the Chief Of Staff was unmistakable. He leant forward, the bulk of his navy Crombie concealing his armour beneath.   In a soft Donegal voice, he asked if I'd help carry Dinny's coffin.

'It's a great honour to carry a comrade,' he said. 'A great honour indeed.'

September and Home from Hospital

Gnarled sticks.
Complex route of living veins.
Bare and beautiful, your limbs
Quiver and shake away
The last clothes of summer.

Clear glass.
Changing picture frame.
Through you, autumn comes.
Red berries, dark wood.
Grey, insipid sky.
Warmth of homemade broth.

Changes

The guilty thoughts circled through my head. It was all my fault. 'Why hadn't I listened to him when he said he didn't feel too well? Oh why had I insisted that he clean up the mess he had made?' My poor Derek lying in a hospital bed and it was all my fault. So he had a party while I was away and wrecked the house but I had insisted he clean the house from top to bottom. I didn't listen to him when he said he felt rotten. Then when I sent him upstairs to tidy the bathroom he collapsed. ' What good is a clean bathroom if my son is really ill?' I had called an ambulance and he was whisked away for tests as soon as we got to the hospital. Here I was pacing the corridors and drinking weak coffee while he was in such pain. He'd been in there such a long time. It must be really serious.

Oh, to think I'd called him a layabout and told him to get off his lazy behind and get a job. He was a good boy really. I wouldn't even make him breakfast. Told him he had to learn how to cook for himself. That might have been his last meal. What if he died? What kind of mother am I? My poor boy. I wonder what is taking the doctors so long? I go outside and light a cigarette inhaling deeply.

What kind of mother am I? I ask myself again. Derek had moaned he had gotten stung by a wasp. My reply had been that I'd gotten stung plenty of times and still managed to cook and clean. Am I too hard-hearted? I ask myself. I vow that if Derek comes home from this hospital, things will change. I'll look after him and cook all his meals and even give up work if he needs me. There will never be another cross word between us. I'll be the nicest, most understanding mother in the world. I decide to go back inside and find the doctor.

The doctor comes out looking harassed and tired. He must have been working hard on Derek.

'How is he doctor?' I ask.

'Come through and see for yourself,' the doctor replies leading me through the double doors. There is Derek lying on the bed smiling up at a pretty nurse. He looks absolutely normal to me. Thank God.

'What was wrong doctor? Will I need to look after him at home in case he has a funny turn again? I can give up work and make sure he is never left alone in case he has a relapse' I say to the doctor. The doctor looks vaguely puzzled and says:

'I don't think there will be any need for that. Your son is in perfect health. He just collapsed from over indulging in alcohol this weekend. He didn't drink enough water and was a bit dehydrated, that's all. He has been asleep for the past two hours and we couldn't wake him. Now could you kindly take him home as there are really sick people who need the bed?'

I turn to glance at Derek and he says:

'I'm starving, Mum. Any chance you would take me out and treat me to dinner?'

'Wait until I get you home you cheeky sod,' I reply. 'You can finish cleaning the house and if you think I will be running around after you you're wrong. Get out to the car,' I say hitting him on the head with my handbag. 'You lazy sod, wasting doctors time like that. Wait until I get you home. Things are going to change...'

Different Worlds

Today you walked out
Into the pouring rain
No coat, hat or umbrella
From the window
I kept watch
As you paced up and down the road
You returned
Knocked on your own door
And asked, 'May I come in?'
I took your hand
You pushed me back
Shouted, 'No'
And walked away again
Back into the rain
I shook my head
nothing left to say
My only hope that in your world
The sun shines for you today
You wanted to dry the cups you said
I gave you the towel
Next minute
You were wearing it
On top of your head
I smiled
You did too
Are these now the only connections
Between me and you?
Oh! Patience I pray.
Alzheimer
It is you
That's holding her hand
And leading her astray.

The Repatriate

He stepped onto the platform, looked around him and sighed. He watched his exhaled breath misting in the air. He buttoned up his worn coat and then rubbed his hands furiously. Then he smirked *home sweet home.* There was no one to collect him. They didn't know he was coming.

God, has it been sixteen years... He remembered the day he left perfectly – standing on this platform; his mam, sniffling, fighting against tears.

'Be careful Johnny, we love you. We love you so much. Ke-ke-keep in touch...' she couldn't continue, emotion overcoming her. And he remembered his dad holding her and looking on with a mixture of pride and sorrow at his departing teenage boy; his lips pressed firm as Johnny boarded the train.

He was desperate at maintaining contact. *Poor Mam.* He had good intentions but living nomadically on foreign soil had defeated him. He didn't want to disappoint them.

Dear Mam and Dad, how are ye? Well, I hate it here. They treat us with contempt and we do the same to them. It's hard to find work and it's never secure. We follow it as best we can but sometimes I just want to say, 'to hell with this.' Sometimes the bastards don't even pay us. I don't bother with mass anymore and God knows when I last confessed... He couldn't even write it if he tried.

The fairy lights that adorned the local businesses twinkled but bar a new house here and there, the place was still bleak. The buildings were still old and crumbling. That heavy air of poverty and depression still hung around.

He passed the snooker hall and wondered what the old gang were up to. God he loved that place. They used to loiter there for hours – playing, smoking, and laughing. Himself and the Murphy twins were great for sharking strangers and making a quick penny. He felt a twinge of guilt again; Paul and J.J. Murphy, his two best friends. Paul was charming, self-assured and amusing. J.J. was subdued, the quieter twin, but he was generous and loyal. Though they were small for their age, the two would never back down in a fight and they would never let any harm come to Johnny.

Johnny remembered an incident in primary school in which Father Carney, an ill tempered, aggressive man, once tackled Johnny. He wrote the sentence:

'Mysteries are truths above reason, which we are to believe even though we cannot comprehend them.' He repeated it.

'Now, class, repeat the sentence.'

The class recited it.

'Now you, John, you read it.'

Johnny looked at the board. All he could see were squiggles and lines. He tried to recall what they had repeated but it wouldn't come. He pleaded with his memory. Nothing. He stared at the board. Nothing.

'You can't read the sentence?' Carney was at his desk immediately, wide-eyed with rage.

'N-n-no sir.'

'You liar, you sinner. I have had my eye on you. I know your likes. I can't read it he says. I tell you this much; you won't lie to me again.'

He raised his fist at Johnny and struck him in the jaw. The impact of the blow knocked Johnny from his seat and blood poured from his mouth. Carney stood over him, with his foot aimed sadistically at Johnny's head. The Murphys protested straight away.

'Leave him alone, leave him alone!' J.J. frantically shouted. Carney barely noticed him.

Paul snarled: 'Leave him alone Carney, quick J.J. get Father Flynn.'

J.J. glanced at the door and rose out of his seat. Carney shot over to where the Murphys sat. Behind him lay a sprawled, bleeding child and moments later there were two more casualties. He broke J.J.'s thumb by twisting it until the crack of the bone was heard. Johnny shuddered at remembering that sound. Paul suffered more; his nose was pounded four times before he passed out from the pain. Mrs. Murphy never sent them to school again.

All my fault.

Johnny cringed at the memory as he continued his walk through the town. He noticed a speck on his jacket, then another, then more. He raised his hands up. Snow. Though it was cold and miserable, Johnny always felt there was something heart warming about snow at Christmas time. *I'm home for Christmas.* It was something he'd promised for years. He was excited again about surprising his parents. They'd be almost heading to bed.

As he turned the corner, wrapped up in his thoughts, he heard his name shouted. He looked around, curiously.

'Over here, Johnny, over here!'

He could just about make out two figures, sitting on the crossroads' wall. He walked towards them, his heart quickening.

'Johnny ya dog.'

'J.J.? Paul?' he queried.

'Ya, who else sure!' Paul responded.

'Oh my God lads, I, Jesus, how, it's been ages, look at ye, God above.' Johnny gazed at the two of them. They looked fresh and young.

'Ye haven't aged a bit lads,' he commented as his rubbed his own hard, wrinkled skin.

'Ah will ya stop, ya faggot!' J.J. joked. 'So you came home.... at last. We've been waiting ages to see ya!'

'I'm sorry about that, lads. I know. I'm terrible. It would take ages to save and then before ya know it, ya'd need the money for something else. I haven't been in touch with Mam and Dad either but sure God knows I can't read or write. I'm like the prodigal son; well at least I'm hoping for a similar welcome return'

'They won't mind,' Paul said, 'they'll be so happy to see ya - a bit like ourselves. So Johnny, tell us what's been going on since we last met.'

Johnny started. He released the thoughts that had been haunting his mind. It had been so long since he had a proper conversation with anyone, it all spewed out of him - his loneliness, his depression, his unsettled life. Finally, he realised the time and his manners.

'Sorry lads, look at me, talking non-stop and all about me. Didn't ask ye nothing, how's things with ye?'

'Johnny, from the sounds of it, you needed to get that off your chest. And would ya stop sure there's nothing new with us; we've been here all along,' said J.J.

'Married?' Johnny enquired.

'Nah, we never found the right women. All the decent ones moved on eventually.'

'What about Kathleen? Herself and yourself were solid for awhile.'

'True,' J.J. answered, 'but it wasn't meant to be. Though I'll always look out for her.'

'God it's been an age lads.' Johnny said with regret.

'Ya, really, we've been waiting to see you for so long. We're delighted! But Johnny, ya know, your mam and da aren't going to be up for much longer. You better head off home,' warned Paul.

'Jes, you're right.'

'I am always right!' Paul replied.

Johnny laughed.

'Right so fellas, a game of snooker tomorrow evening and we'll catch up right. A couple of pints after. Loser pays!'

'We'd really love that, really would Johnny. We felt awful bad that we never said goodbye,' Paul said.

'Ara stop lads, it was a spur of the moment thing, ye know how it is. Can't wait to see the auld pair. Good luck,' Johnny shouted as he walked away.

'We'll see ya Johnny. You take it easy.' J.J. whispered.

Johnny crossed the slushy road. Despite the soft melting on his hair and ears he didn't feel cold. He whistled as he drew near to his home. The lights were still on in the cottage and he had a quick peek in the window. His dad was at the hearth, burying the embers of the fire. His mam was busying herself around the kitchen, making sure everything was in order. There was a small Christmas tree in the corner with little boxes wrapped underneath. Johnny stretched his arm to the top of the window frame and fumbled until he found the spare key. He let himself in the front door but knocked on the kitchen door. He opened it gently and peered in. His parents were looking at him at first with curiosity, then with recognition and delight.

'Johnny!' his mother exclaimed, her eyes and mouth opened wide. 'Come in, come in will ya.' She ushered him in and it was like nothing had changed. She grabbed onto his soaked coat, 'oh you'll catch your death boy, take that off.'

His father smiled broadly and shook his hand. 'Jesus son, look at ya. All grown up and strong. And the image of your grandfather.'

They sat in the kitchen for hours. His mother gossiped. His father talked about the G.A.A. and his predictions for the county team in next year's championship and their progress in the years of Johnny's absence.

'Well son, do ya want to go out for a few scoops tomorrow night?' his father asked.

'I dunno Dad; maybe, but I kind of already made plans.'

'Really Johnny, isn't that great. What'll you be going at?' His mother's nose scrunched up towards her eyes with the question.

'Well, I actually met up with the lads on the walk from the station. With J.J. and Paul. Had a great chat. Think we're going for a game of snooker and drinks after,' Johnny said, already excited at the prospect.

Silence.

Johnny noticed that the room seemed colder now, he rubbed his hands together. He looked at his parents. His fathers face had become ashen and serious. Tears welled in the eyes of his mother.

Dead silence.

Johnny was confused. 'What'd I say?'

They glanced at each other worriedly.

'You didn't hear?' his mother spoke quietly.

'Hear what?' Johnny was uneasy and shifted on his stool.

His father piped up, 'John, about ten years ago there was an awful accident. There was a cattle truck, headed to the mart. The twins were sitting on the wall at the high crossroads waiting for their lift to work. The truck driver skidded and well, he lost control of his vehicle. He smashed into the wall. It was a terrible tragedy.'

'What d'ya mean? What are you saying?' Johnny asked.

74

His mother put her arm around him, 'Johnny, J.J. and Paul are dead. Died when they were young men. We thought you would have known, heard it somehow, somewhere when you were gone.'

The Gathering

Is this some royal feast?
The guests have come in their hundreds.
A secret get-together that no trumpets heralded.
Who sent out the invitations?
They're here in black dress-suits
Stately, tall and proud.
Others in glamorous white, gliding elegantly,
Others have speckle-breasted bodies of glory.

Together they enjoy the richness of scent so sweet.
The invitation sent by Mother Nature
Wafting off on a gentle breeze,
Entrancing for miles the birds upon the wing to come.
The meadow cut down in her prime
To lie in piles upon the ground.
Its sweetness too, to die, inside it.

The guests are here then
To wake the grass, and celebrate
The cutting of the harvest, and to
Nourish themselves on the juicy leftovers
Now uncovered and, as all is eaten
They fly away and the meadow is left to die in peace.

Winter Calls

October is here again. September has just passed and the leaves are falling steadily off the trees. They gather endlessly, covering the footpaths like a blanket. Blackberries have ripened and are in full bloom. The birds have come and some have gone to faraway lands like the swallows to South Africa, leaving the Bushes scantily clad.

Ma puts the jam jars in the oven, tumbles in the blackberries, sugar and lemon rind into her aluminium pot and stirs in wonder and anticipation. Everybody loves her jam, especially the neighbours to whom she gives a jar at Christmas. At breakfast Dad dips his knife into the jar of its sticky sweetness, swiping his buttered bread. My tongue waters as I chew on a morsel.

Frogs lay their spawn in marshy lands and baby frogs are hatched. They, in brown or green with darker green spots, hop through an open door and are often to be found in the oddest of places in the kitchen or sitting room. Lizards emerge from the unlikeliest of places and may be found in the corner of a room or under the telly.

The days shorten, nights lengthen. Rain continues to pour on an already swamped bog which turns sodden. The air chills. Jumpers are pulled from the back of the wardrobe and find form. Thermal vests are the mode. Fires light early in the morn. Logs are thrown on the hearth with sods and twigs. The oil lorry trails from one house to another refueling tanks for the following few months. Winter is here once again!

A Bicycle Ride

We set off from Up The Glen
on our brand new whiz bang bicycles.
Silver, sleek and shiny,
and a perfect little showcase
for a skinny little,
pretty little, blonde girl.
Me. I'm a fraud.
Ample buttocks spilling over saddle
My aunt. She's round like me,
but she can ride a bike.
Legs sailing round effortlessly, peddles dancing carefree.
As I push on. Determined and distressed.

On we go though, Out The Road.
I can use the gears now, the sea breeze lovely on my face.
We pass a clucking couple,
their late and treasured gift, tottering and toddling.
They feel blessed, like me, on a tranquil evening.
We pass the spotless, well-designed beach bungalows
of architects and merchants.
And their beautiful educated children.
I am not intimidated though.
I'm educated too you know.
And I go cycling on shiny bikes on pleasant evenings.

And Round The Shore we go. We don't turn back,
all encompassed by the gifts bequeathed by birthplace.
Island views, cascading hills and castle ruins calling out to sea.
Silky water rolling onto rocks beside the road.
Streetlights glow amber in The Village.
I need to go Up The Glen. In daylight,
in honeysuckle, streams and friendly neighbours.
Reluctantly we turn.

I can't get the gears right.
My legs are wading concrete,
but I feel good.
I feel real and good.
I don't give up –
I climb Croagh Patrick.
I stick to diets.
And on mild autumn evenings
I cycle by the sea.
Where I was born,
Where my people are.
And I can hold my own.

Mistresses

Chipped red nails scratch a hairy back,
Plunge into flesh weeping sweat.
And she is crushed,
Stained.
Maintained by the pay
She waits for it,
Soaked in him.
Raw,
Picking skin from behind
Her chipped red nails.

Smooth strokes of red are painted carefully
By a soft ornamented hand.
Palm outstretched,
Bored.
Money is bestowed
Unquestioned.
For him she is always pretty,
Polished.
Admiring her elegant nails, though
They are not hers.

The Russian Doll

Number 1 sat there on the shelf wondering why no one had admired her in the last couple of days. Usually someone came into the room or passed by and thought how cute they all looked standing in a row, or put them inside each other and admired how well the other four fitted into her. But for days, nobody. She sat on the shelf in the bedroom, a room she had watched go from pink fairies, to posters of singers and bands, to a computer and stereo, to, most recently, her owner spending hours studying. But no owner, no owner's mother or any of the bands of friends that spent hours sitting on the bed laughing, crying or talking depending on the day. Usually one of them took the Russian dolls from the shelf and stacked and unstacked them into each other absentmindedly. She loved being handled and admired, which was why she was wondering why no one had come near her for days. There were still people in the house because she could hear them through the door but no one came near her.

I wonder, she thought if I were smaller would someone notice me. I mean, I am the largest and when we are stacked together and people open me they all exclaim when they see Number 2 and say how clever she is to be hiding. Yes she's slimmer and cuter then me so I think I will make myself be Number 2 and surely the next person passing by will notice how cute I am on the shelf, or come in and stack us together and exclaim when Number 2 appears when Number 1 is opened. So she wished and wished with all her might. 'I will be Number 2. I will be Number 2' And she was. Now she thought I'll be the one that amazes people how I can fit inside Number 1. So she sat there and sat there and sat there. But after a week no one had come near her.

Maybe if I were Number 3, I'd be noticed. Everyone thinks we are all the same but the middle one is a little prettier then the rest of us. She's also in the middle, not too big like Number 1 and not too small like Number 5, but just right in the middle and the two each side of her just show her off as being the perfect one in the middle. If you look from either the right or the left, you always see her as the important one. So she thought she would be the one in the middle for a while. It was harder to change herself this time as her power had diminished with her size. But she concentrated really hard. 'I will be Number 3. I will be Number 3. I will be Number 3.' And she was. Now I'll just sit here and wait to be admired as the perfect one, the one in the middle. Not too big and not too small and definitely the prettiest. So she stood there, in the middle, for over a week and no one came near her to notice that she was prettier then the other 4.

Maybe being in the middle isn't the best position after all, she thought. I think Number 4 has the best of all worlds. Small enough to be cute and make 3, 2, and 1 look like great big hulks but not the pathetic baby at the end, either. Yea and when we're stacked together and someone unstacks us, they will really *oh and ah* by the time they get to Number 4,because they don't know where it's going to end. So I'm sure I'd get noticed, if I was Number 4. So once again she started to wish herself different. 'I will be Number 4. I will be Number 4. I will be Number 4. I will be Number 4.' She really had to concentrate this time. And she was. She sat there on the shelf waiting to be admired, waiting for someone to stack the dolls together and then unstack and be amazed by her as Number 4.

After two weeks of no one looking at her, she started thinking again. Everyone loves the baby. No matter how many times we get stacked and unstacked, it's always the baby that gets the most attention. She gets handled like she's delicate and fragile and pretty and cute and special. I've been the biggest for so long it would be great to be the baby, the cute one, the one that doesn't have to be responsible for all the others, the one that everyone notices and wants to protect. I really want to try and see if being Number 5 makes people notice me and love me. So she really concentrated. ' I will be Number 5. I will be Number 5. I will be Number 5. I will be Number 5. I will be Number 5.' And she was. Now I'm the baby and I will be everyone's favourite and as soon as the next person passes the open door they will come in and admire me and wonder aloud at my daintiness and cuteness.

She only got to stand there for a few days when people came into the room. She recognised the voice of one as the voice she had most heard over time. 'Yea Mom I know I promised to clean my

82

room up before I left, but you know what I'm like. I didn't realise the job would keep me so busy and Dublin is such fun and I've made loads of new friends. I can't wait to show you the apartment I got. Its great, but it needs some of my bits and pieces to make it feel like home. Oh look, my Russian dolls. Do you remember when you got me these and I spent ages stacking and unstacking them, hiding one inside the other again and again? I used to think they were great when I was a kid. You know I think I'll take them with me to Dublin, they'll remind me of home. But the apartment is a bit small so I can't display them all in a row like that. No I'll stack them one inside each other and that's how they will sit on the shelf.' So she took Number 5 and put her inside Number 4 and put them inside Number 3 and them inside Number 2 and them inside Number 1.

Number 5 could have cried. She had used all her energy and power getting to Number 5 so she could be the most admired one. But now she was destined to be hidden deep inside, for who knew how long, the Number one: the one she had always been – would get to sit on the new shelf, to be admired and watch the world.

Boy

Tallish and dark,
And oh so fine,
Is this guy I met,
Blue eyes sparkling,
Smiling, laughing, at my foolish babblings,
Eyes meet eyes, stomach flutters,
Cheeks burn.

I saw him sitting, proud and tall,
On his magnificent steed.
He smiled, we chatted,
I tentative at first, till we find a common ground,
And on that I seize.
He likes horses, well obviously,
He does opera, and I think that's cool!

Fruits of War

MiYa Fahed looked at the young man in front of her and felt like spitting on him, but she new her place and avoided trouble – she no longer had the fervour to fight. She dragged her left foot and envisioned a hail of bullets piercing his back, and herself behind the metal with a grin on her face. When did the antagonism start she wondered. Look at him now - poking his rifle at the checkpoint, muttering and sniggering.

Her shoulders were hunched by the weight of her basket, and her step criss-crossed as she tried to drag herself forward. She flinched for a few seconds when he brought his hands up to feel her body. He could not see behind her veil what she was muttering but his eyes could read hers. He sensed her hatred and because of this, he jammed his fist into her side and kicked her forward.

She stood up, wiped the red sand from her lip and tried with every muscle not to flinch. She arched her back, held her nose to the sky and kept her dignity. Only once she reached the corner did she allow herself to bend forward and let the pain take hold of her.

Approaching from the same direction was a group of singing soldiers. Their joviality brought a chill to her thoughts as she recognised one of their voices. So she crossed the street and waddled around another corner. She would have to take the long way now.

Making a left turn she gulped a little, closed her eyes tightly and forced herself to shut out the memory of this street. Years divided her and this part of town. Flashes of faces and gunshots wounded her thoughts. She was not going to cry, she was beyond that now. She opened her eyes pulled her shoulders back and kept her eyes on Centre Street.

Then without warning the smell of fishmongers crawled into her nostrils like manna and beckoned her on. She stopped at the first stall and haggled herself a fresh mackerel for no other reason than to rest for a while. She walked on and bumped her way through the crowd unaware that the mackerel had slipped out onto the dusty red gravel. Exactly the same down here as it was on the East side of Pakistan. Here and there, standing out from the crowd, were foreign women in pants. Those women beckon trouble, she thought, flaunting their faces and exposing themselves to men. She had spent years in London working as a translator trying to fit in. But the longer she stayed the more her eyes revealed the evil intentions of the western world.

Drunken women, prostituting for husbands, claiming innocence after being raped. Mothers drinking with their children, then wondering why their offspring amount to nothing. Their eternal search for false perfection and capitalism was the reason so many youngsters turned to gangsterism. She felt safe inside her burka, and pitied them.

The noise of people haggling their wants and the stale smell of heated bodies wafted their way through the market place. The deep furrows across her brow shifted and for the first time in many years she felt how good it was to smile.

Two hours after closing her front door she reached the bullet ridden hospital. Lightened in spirit she let the guard do his routinely poking of her fruit basket. She stretched her face into a wider grin and showed her crooked teeth that were somehow untouched by decay. She offered him an orange from the top.

'Here Josef – today it's for free.'

Up the stairs she went – leaving Josef open mouthed and silent. Never had he seen MiYa give anything for free.

She wandered the seven corridors keeping her eye on the clock at each reception. No time for witty backchat today, she wanted to be home with her scrapbook and her cat. A good day – she had sold all the fruit.

She glanced at the clock and it seemed to click louder as it neared 7pm. She would have to leave now if she wanted to be home before dark. The seconds rang in her throat as she hurried to the door and down the steps. Four miles is a long way home at her age. Her leg was heavy, and in her haste, she tumbled down a few steps. She knew she was not going to get any help from Josef, so she ignored his sniggering, clenched her teeth and tried to pull herself up.

The sweat was pouring into her eyes when suddenly a thundering bang knocked her down again. She turned around in time to see Josef's expression change as his laughter echoed and was drowned by the explosion. Blood oozed from his nostrils as all around him shrapnel danced. 'Bang!' Adrenalin pumped her up and she crawled her way across the street. Something made her slump against the building behind the safety of the wall. She saw the mayhem falling over Josef's kneeled body as soldiers and civilians united in their fear, tried to run from the uncertainty.

Frozen in confusion time slowed down and with ringing in her ears she witnessed the symphony. 'Three...... four....five......six.......' was she counting correctly or had the terrifying beauty of dust and gore and blood controlled her. She watched as some scrambled out the building – and others crawled to safety. No more the brave taunting of earlier, instead distorted fear contorted Josef's face. She watched in silence until the beating in her throat slowed to a familiar pace. How many explosions were there, she wondered?

She picked up courage and dragged her bleeding body up. She moved past the wave of screaming creatures up the steps. The pain was lost on her as her broken leg dragged over the fallen debris. She had survived this madness of war. How many lives did she have left out of this cursed cat-like existence? Crying and crippled with pain, she dragged her body deeper and deeper into the crumbling building. When she could go no further she stretched her arms out and panted her defiance to Allah. Now, let this Hindu blood end where it started.

And it came. The white walls pulled away from their ancient seams and folded inwards. Brown golden dust crashing downwards and then exploding upwards towards heaven. Her body wedged between a soldier and a filing cabinet, where they pulled her out. Blood around her temples and a broken leg were the only signs that she had even been in the air raid, said a reporter into the television camera's. A miracle, an absolute miracle read the headlines.

To Get Away

Lying here eyes closed
I feel the sun's warm satin sheet
Coving me
The soft damp bed of grass
Underneath me
Dawns chorus echo around me
All light and happy.

Hard ground
Thumps and shakes
Faceless people rushing round
Walking through you as if you are a ghost
Dark and grey
It's good to get away.

School

A sea of blue grey and maroon,
Crowded dark corridors,
Each one opening to a different room,
Inside a different personality.
Some are chatty some are snappy,
Some are boring some are mean,
Some are kind and one is just outright eccentric.
Each one making us work.

A school of girls,
Chatty, and bitchy, quiet and some so very mean,
Skinny, tall, short or fat and some in between.
Happy, sad, angry or mad,
So many personalities and types,
Some fights along the way,
Each and every day,
Cooped up in this school.

Standing in the Gap
For Breege

Fine thing.
Farmer?
Will he ask me
To dance?

Dreaming of
Wild flower strewn meadows
Playing with fluffy white lambs
Sunny, fresh air days
Long legged new calves
Hand in hand
Walking the fields

Marriage
Children
Lots of land
Little money
Long, wet, cold, days
Picking up tractor parts
Dropping animals to marts

Lambs needing bottles
Calves needing buckets
Silage to be forked
He needs his dinner

Romantic walks
Yea right
Hey I'm moving the cows
Will you stand in the gap?

Alone

Helen lay back in the long luscious green grass. Tears misted her eyes. She was oblivious to the sound of the birds singing and the breeze whispering through the trees. She hugged the urn tightly to her chest.

'How could you go and leave me all alone?' she whispered. 'We vowed we would always stay together and now you're gone and I'm all alone. How can I go on without you? You were my reason for living, breathing and getting up each day.' The tears were running down her cheeks faster and faster. ' I feel so guilty. Why did I turn my back on you at that moment? That car was speeding and hit you. It should have been me, not you' she cried. 'I tried to save you but it was to late.' She lay back down in the grass and sighed. It was too late now. Brian was gone for good. The time had come to say goodbye.

Standing up she slowly walked towards the lake. The view of the faraway hills and mountains was spectacular. It had been their special place. A secluded area that no one else knew about. A piece of paradise to call their own. 'Now you can be free' she said. Raising her arm she turned the urn upside down and watched as the ashes fell in to the water. Wiping a tear from her eye she trudged slowly home. Brian was at peace now. He was free in the water. The place he had loved most in his short life. She would never forget how he used to enjoy jumping into that lake and splashing around.

Nearing her home she blew her nose and straightened her shoulders. Enough was enough. She had grieved for long enough. It was time to get on with her life. She'd never forget Brian; he would always be in her heart. She was greeted at the door by her husband Max. There, lying at his feet was a beautiful golden Labrador pup.

'I know how upset you are about Brian' he said softly. ' So I thought this fella might cheer you up.'

'Oh Max, he's beautiful. Thank you so much' she cried. 'He can sleep in Brian's kennel.'

Split Second

It only takes a minute
or less.
No, more like a second
or less
and it's all over.

They were going to pick up a ladder,
collect a son,
watch a match,
drive to church.
Going somewhere.

Was it
the sun that blinded,
the road slippery with rain,
the wind that blew the branch,
the dog that distracted?

Who knows what or how?
A life of seconds, minutes, hours,
days, weeks, years,
moments.
Gone.

Accident is a long word
for a split second.
A short word
for a life
extinguished.

The Lines of Life

Riding home on the train last week, I watched an elderly lady sitting to the right in front of me. I could just see her profile. Her face was a city of characters. She must have at least been in her 70's, with a long, not so easy life in behind her. She sat there, casually glancing at different people as she stuffed small pieces of bread into her mouth. Frequently her hand would dive into the plastic bag on her lap, and fish out another morsel of bread. Her hands were weatherworn, scrubby and tanned.

Her face imaged her appearance. She had a large hooked nose and a very large mole on her left cheek, which of course was the only side visible to me. There was not an inch of smooth skin to be seen, only large crevices of time. With each bite, her face seemed to collapse upwards. Her cheekbones rose to form extended round bags, which of course was crowned with that very obvious mole. The massive movement of her face was caused by the lack of teeth. Her eyes darted around her. Occasionally she would turn her head and look back at the people, as if she was looking for something or someone. Her old leather coat was badly in need of a dry clean as was the rest of her. Each and every aspect of her portrayed, age and hardship. I wondered how a person like her managed to survive. Her lack of cleanliness made me feel uncomfortable, yet, at the same time, fascinated. Here was a person who most probably was not as old as she appeared who had done her time, not in years, but in the quality of years. She most probably could keep the entire occupants on this train entertained with her life story. I observed her further, averting my eyes every time she looked over her shoulders.

Her untidy woollen skirt hung ragged around her legs. Short, dirty grey socks protruded out of discoloured runners. The skin of her legs matched her hands and face, scratched and flaky. I did not like the look of this lady; her lack of hygiene was disturbing to others. Shortly before my stop, she turned around and caught my eye. Her mouth did not stop the constant chewing, her face collapsing and readjusting continuously. She looked directly into my eyes. At first I thought she did not register, but slowly her features changed. Her face seemed to expand sideways; a brilliant gummy smile appeared, changing my total opinion of her. There she was, the old ragged lady, with the crevice face, the filthy fingers, the scarf tied tightly around her large head. Her mole rising and falling in beat with her gums. Here was an old person; wise with age and the most beautiful face I have ever seen. The smile radiated from within her eyes and one forgot the dirt, and only saw the sunshine.

Going West

I sat on a stall shelf under the arcade in South Great George's Street in Dublin, for what seemed like years. I took my place among lots of bits and pieces, teapots, cups, jugs, coffee pots, to mention a few. One day a woman pointed in my direction. The stall attendant moved along the shelf, the woman shaking her head in saying 'no', then placing his finger on my head, she nodded. I was removed from my shelf, left on the table right in front of this woman. She picked me up, looked me over, removed my lid and even looked at my bottom. They exchanged a few words; the woman hesitated, took another look at me and exclaimed

'I'll take it so for the six pounds.' Into a plastic bag and off I go. I travelled a bit, later removed from the bag, given a beautiful warm sudsy bath, dried and polished until my delph shone. I was given place of honour on the corner shelf in her dining room, where I was admired on a regular basis, looked at, pointed to, even removed every now and then to show me off to friends.

I always thought myself to be beautiful, but now, human beings were saying it as well. I loved the way my cap just clicked onto the hook; everyone said this was very unusual. They loved the coloured floral displays I had on my front and back and even one on my lid.

After a number of years of having been lovingly cared for and admired, I was removed from my perch but this time, not put back. What was going on, I asked myself.

'Bubble wrap it and pack it into a shoebox,' she said. Is it me they're talking about? I guess so for I am now cooped up in a box.

One day I heard a guy say: 'These are going west' and off I go again. I travelled for what seemed like hours; there were a few nasty bumps along the way. I felt crushed, but no one seemed to care. I was not checked on. Following a rough ride I was removed from the van with other boxes. Days passed, lots of movement, more chatter. I recognise a voice beside me. The box lid removed, bubble wrap opened back, two big eyes stare in on me, when I hear:

95

'Oh my God, my jug, it's in smithereens.' I'm taken from the box piece by piece and put on the kitchen table. With my lid still intact she went from wall to wall, shelf to shelf, trying to find a suitable spot to leave it on. Eventually, the lid was left on a shelf in the kitchen; she sat back and admires it. A few phone calls were made, enquiring about a delph stitcher, whatever that is. Anyway, not one to be found. I'm was collected into the bubble wrap and back into the box. This separation from my lid was so unfair.

Another time lapse brought me back to the kitchen table to be analysed. Piece by piece I was removed and placed on a tray as she gently tried to match my floral displays. Bits stuck with tacky stuff she called glue – very unpleasant.

'You're wasting your time in that,' someone tells her.

'Well,' she replied, 'I'm having a go.'

Days and weeks passed, little bits of sticking together done every now and then. I'm talked about, looked at, discussed by family members and every visitor that enters the house. By then I had lost interest in this painful experience. I thought I was sinking into depression.

The day the sun shone on me through the kitchen window was a new awakening. I felt a bit alive again; I started to take notice; my lid was still on the shelf, and I was feeling quite different than I had for a very long time. I had a good gander at myself – the excitement. My body had taken shape once more, floral displays and all. I was so afraid to get over excited for fear of bursting all these new seams I had. I knew by the expression on my owner's face, that she too was overjoyed. A little later that week, more excitement – my lid was removed from the shelf and very gently clicked to my hook, as if she feared my body might collapse under the weight of it. Only then did I learn that a few pieces, too shattered to put together, were left out, leaving a hole in my back. What the heck, hole in my back or not, this lady did not seem to mind, I was once again, displayed, looked at, admired, talked about, even more than ever before. I was restored to my place of honour, this time, behind a lovely glass door. Now I'm not taken out as often, but not for the want of admiring glances. I am still beautiful and can take my place on any shelf or dresser.

It's almost 25 years since I travelled from Dublin. I was made redundant about four years ago after my accident and thanks to my owner I'm still lovingly cared for. Just two weeks ago, she removed me from my shelf, took me to the kitchen table; she left the room and returned with a small box and started looking through it and making shapes at me. Hell, I thought what's going on here? She then started to snap me, taking pictures from every direction. This embarrassed me a bit as I'm not very photogenic.

I couldn't get my head around this; I wanted to crack up on all my seams again.

After 20 years of being perfect, she now snaps me!

Aren't human beings very strange characters?

Life in Eighteen Words

Bred Born Bigger
Meet Marry Mate
Father Mother Childer
Fulfilled Fun Frolics
Work Worry Weary
Dig Deep Die

Writers

Celia Anderson's daughter, Jacqueline, inspired her humorous animal stories. Author of "Collection of Tails" and articles for www.castlebar.ie, Celia was born in Switzerland, raised in South Africa and lives in Ireland.

Monica Browne lives near Claremorris. She has recently joined the Mayo Writers' Block. The inspiration for her poems and short stories comes through her love of nature and rural Ireland.

Eileen Byrne comes from Claremorris. She is an avid reader of books and was fascinated by them as a child. She admires Pearse, Yeats and Kavanagh.

Teresa Coleman is a native of Balla currently living near Claremorris. She studied English and History at college and is a secondary school teacher. Her interests include reading, theatre, cinema and psychology. She writes poetry and short stories.

John Corless is a founder member of the Mayo Writers' Block. He writes short stories, drama and some poetry.

Áine Egan is 30 years old. Originally from the north Antrim coast, she grew up in Australia and lives in Claremorris with her husband and her dog Snowy.

Paula Gilbert has been a member of the Mayo Writers' Block' for two years. When she's not busy running after her four lively children she enjoys writing short stories and reading.

Chloe Hughes is a second-year student who enjoys reading, playing music and creative writing. A member of the Mayo Writers' Block since the beginning, this is her first publication.

Lucie Kavanagh lives in Ballyhaunis and works for Western Care Association. She loves reading music and poetry and spends her time making a derelict house not quite so derelict.

Joyce Kirrane lives in Claremorris. She studied film and television and has a special interest in screen writing. Her favourite director is David Lynch.

Jimmy Lardner is a native of Belclare, Co. Galway. He has lived in Claremorris for the past thirty-five years where he is employed by the ESB.

Margaret Leahy has been writing in her head all her life and started putting poems and stories on paper when she joined the group, as her head was full.

Sinead McGhee has been a member of Mayo Writers' Block for two years. Her interest lies in poetry and short stories.

Nuala Melia is a poet exploring the inner person. She encapsulates thoughts which are common to all. She also has degrees in English Philosophy and this influences her poetry.

E.M. Reapy is aged 22 and from Claremorris. She writes fiction, fusing various styles and influences in her work. She records contemporary observations on an evolving Irish society.

Geraldine Toughey was born in the north of England. She had her first poem published in the Western People aged 14 and likes writing poetry about emotional situations.

Jessica Warrington is a 19 year-old student from Mount St. Michael's Claremorris. She started writing at a young age.

Copyright Notice

Thanks

The Mayo Writers' Block wishes to sincerely thank Terry McDonagh for his help with this anthology. His official title was editor, but his input was far greater than that.

Thanks also to South West Mayo Leader without whose help this project would never have materialised.

Thanks are also due to Mayo County Council's Arts Office for their help.

Thanks to all the writers who submitted work for consideration.

Finally, thanks to you the reader, we hope you enjoy '*Standing in the Gap* – The Mayo Writers' Block – *An Anthology.*'

The Mayo Writers' Block

The Mayo Writers' Block was formed in March 2004. The group has a steady membership of about twenty writers. We meet twice a month, and read and critique members' work. The material is as diverse as life itself. Critiques are constructive and well received. The atmosphere is always positive and supportive of the artistic process involved in getting coherent thoughts onto the page. If you'd like to join the group, you'd be more than welcome.

Twice annually, we run competitions for our members. Ulster Bank Claremorris has generously sponsored the competitions, which have three categories: poetry, short story and an open section. External judges decide the winners.

You'll find more information on our website: www.mayowriters.org. Thanks.

Published By Sionnach Media